TO: _____

FROM: _____

DATE: _____

For it is God who works in you to will and to act in order to fulfill his good purpose.

Philippians 2:13 NIV

Seek and Find Bible Stories: Old Testament for Kids

An Interactive Christian Book and Fun Bible Activities for Kids 6-8: Bible Study Made Easy

By Jamie Whimsy

Kaleidokids Publishing

Published by KaleidoKids Publishing

Scripture quotations taken from The Holy Bible, New International Version® NIV® Copyright © 1973, 1978, 1984, 2011 by Biblica, Inc.
Used with permission. All rights reserved worldwide.

Cover by Ale @aleprodesign
ISBN: 9798335915717
Printed in United States of America

This book is intended for educational andentertainment purposes, providing families with engaging ways to learn about the Bible together. All efforts have been made to ensure the accuracy of the Bible stories and teachings presented. First Edition [08, 2024]

Father, I thank You for the opportunity to create this book. I pray for Your wisdom and strength to make it a blessing. May it touch every young heart and help them grow in understanding of Your love and mercy. Amen.

A Note From The Author

Hello my friends, welcome to "Seek and Find Bible Stories"!
I hope this book, with its fourteen carefully selected Bible stories, helps you understand more about God's love while having fun!
Before you begin reading, please note that each story has four parts:

- Story Summary: A quick look at what happened and the background.
- Bible Teachings: Lessons from the story that help us think, reflect, pray, and live it out.
- Character Introduction: Information about where the character stands in God's chosen family.
- Seek & Find Items: Objects hidden in the story's illustration for you to find.

To the Parents:

This book is designed to first spark young child's interest with seek and find activities and then deepen their understanding of the Bible through the other parts. So it's recommended to start with the seek and find before exploring the rest of the story, as well as discussing how each teaching might be applied to our lives.

To the Children:

I'm so glad you're reading this book! You're about to learn more about the Bible and God's family while enjoying exciting seek & find activities! Have fun finding the hidden objects in the pictures—they're part of the story too! Just a hint: the hidden objects are the same as in the legends, but they might be rotated a little to make it more fun to search.
I hope you enjoy every page and learn more about how precious you are and how much God cares about you.

With love,
Jamie

Table of Contents

Creation Story
(Genesis 1-2)

My friends, have you ever wondered how the sun, plants, and animals came to be? Who's the creator of our world? The short answer is that God created everything, with mankind being His most special creation. According to the Bible, God created everything in six days, and on the seventh day, He rested from His work. Among God's creations, there are also things we cannot directly see, like order and the freedom of choice given to mankind.

Seek & Find

Sunflower 2X

White lily 3X

Butterfly 4X

Vine 2X

Owl 3X

Snake 2X

Eve was the first woman God created. She was made from one of Adam's ribs to be his helper and wife. They enjoyed living in the Garden of Eden.

From the Creation Story, we learn about God's love for mankind. God created Adam in His image and breathed life into him. Each of us is a wonderful creation of God, and each of our lives has a purpose.

Adam was the first man God created. He lived in the Garden of Eden and named all the animals. God gave him the responsibility to take care of the garden.

Noah's Ark teaches us that our Lord doesn't like wickedness and that there will be consequences for sins. But God will always show mercy and protect those who follow His words and do the right things.

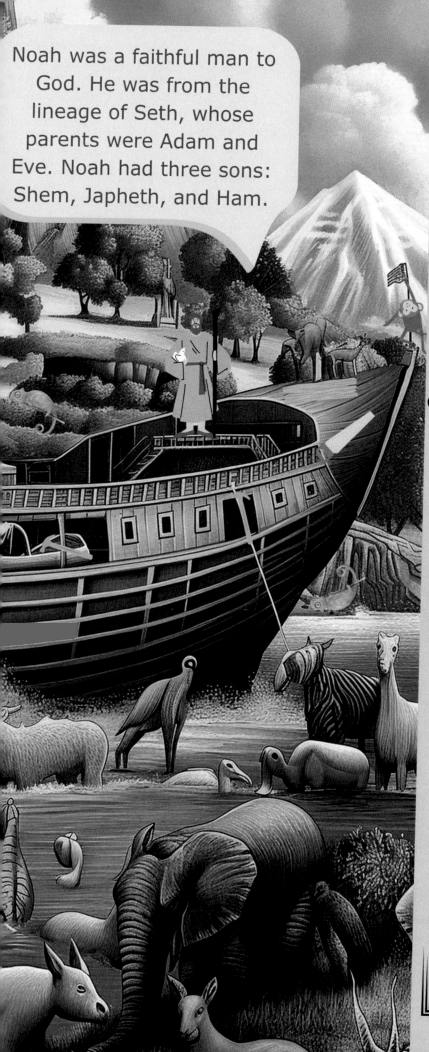

Noah was a faithful man to God. He was from the lineage of Seth, whose parents were Adam and Eve. Noah had three sons: Shem, Japheth, and Ham.

Noah's Ark
(Genesis 6-8)

As we know, Adam and Eve chose to eat the forbidden fruit, so they had to leave the Garden of Eden. This brought sin into the world. As their sons and daughters married and the number of people grew on earth, God saw the wickedness in their hearts and lives and decided to wipe out all mankind in a flood. Still, God showed mercy to Noah and his family by telling Noah to build an ark to survive the great flood, with pairs of each animal.

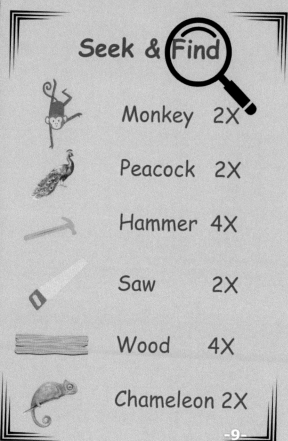

Seek & Find

🐒	Monkey	2X
🦚	Peacock	2X
🔨	Hammer	4X
	Saw	2X
	Wood	4X
🦎	Chameleon	2X

Abraham's Journey
(Genesis 12-13)

God asked Abraham to leave his home for a promised land. Having strong faith in God, Abraham left Harran with his whole family and embarked on a long journey to Canaan, a place he had never seen before. God also promised Abraham numerous offspring like the dust of the earth. Even though he was old and had yet no children, Abraham believed in God's promise.

Seek & Find

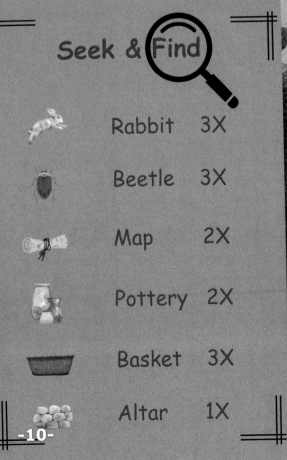

Rabbit	3X
Beetle	3X
Map	2X
Pottery	2X
Basket	3X
Altar	1X

Abraham, a man of great faith, is known as the father of many nations. He was the descendant of Shem and the grandfather of Jacob.

From Abraham's journey, we learn the importance of faith. It teaches us that we should always live by faith, not by sight.

Jacob, the son of Isaac and grandson of Abraham, was given the name 'Israel' by God. He had twelve sons who became the ancestors of the twelve tribes of Israel.

Jacob's Ladder
(Genesis 28)

As instructed by his father, Jacob set out on a trip to look for a wife from one of his relative's home. As it got dark, he lay down in the wilderness and had a wonderful dream. In the dream, Jacob saw a stairway leading up to heaven with angels going up and down, and God stood above giving him blessings. Still immature in his faith in God, Jacob honored that specific place as the 'House of God' and made a few conditional vows.

This story teaches us how to ask for God's help. Yes, we need God's help with many things, but we should not attach any conditions when we pray for His help, as our walk with the Lord is based on faith.

Seek & Find

🐦	Bird	2X
🌼	Flower	4X
✦	Star	4X
🥖	Bread	2X
🪨	Rock	4X
🦋	Butterfly	4X

Joseph Interprets Pharaoh's Dreams
(Genesis 41)

This story teaches us what to do during difficult times or injustice: we should always keep our faith in God. And the Lord will make all things work for our good in the end.

Joseph, the favorite son of Jacob, was sold into slavery in Egypt by his jealous brothers. In Egypt, he suffered more injustice when he was thrown into prison for being righteous. But throughout all the difficulties, Joseph never lost his faith in God and God was also with him. Later, Joseph interpreted Pharaoh's dream with God's help and became the ruler of Egypt, second only to Pharaoh.

Seek & Find

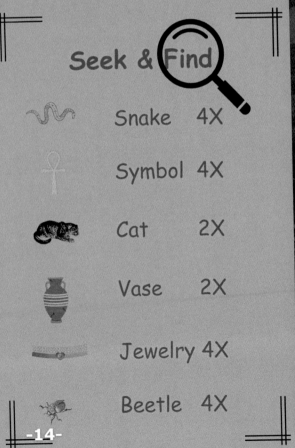

Snake	4X
Symbol	4X
Cat	2X
Vase	2X
Jewelry	4X
Beetle	4X

Moses was a descendant of Abraham and from the tribe of Levi, one of the twelve tribes of Israel. He led the Israelites out of Egypt but didn't get to enter the Promised Land.

> This story teaches us that although we should be humble, we also need to be bold when we hear God's calling in our hearts. We are weak, but we will be made strong with God's presence.

Moses and the Burning Bush
(Exodus 3)

While taking care of sheep near Horeb, Moses saw a bush on fire but didn't burn up. Moses came near for a closer look only to hear God calling his name. God had chosen Moses to lead millions of Israelites out of slavery in Egypt and back to the promised land! At first, Moses didn't think he could do it, but he agreed when God promised to be with him every step of the way.

Seek & Find

Bird   1X

Scroll 2X

Snake   2X

Lizard 2X

The Conquest of Ai
(Joshua 7-8)

After taking Jericho with God's help, the Israelite army led by Joshua thought Ai would be an easy town to capture. However, due to sin they suffered a humiliating defeat with their first attempt. After correcting their mistakes, Joshua and his men carried out God's plan perfectly. They lured the entire Ai army out with a pretended retreat, then had another ambush team attack and take Ai from behind.

Seek & Find

⚔	Sword	3X
╱	Javelin	4X
🕊	Bird	2X
🦎	Lizard	2X
	Smoke	3X
🪲	Beetle	1X

This story teaches us that sins will lead to severe consequences, so we must obey God's words. But if we have sinned, we must ask God's help to deal with our sins to get back on track.

Joshua was from the tribe of Ephraim, one of the twelve tribes of Israel. He became the leader of the Israelites after Moses. Joshua's faith and leadership helped the Israelites defeat their enemies and settle in the Promised Land of Canaan.

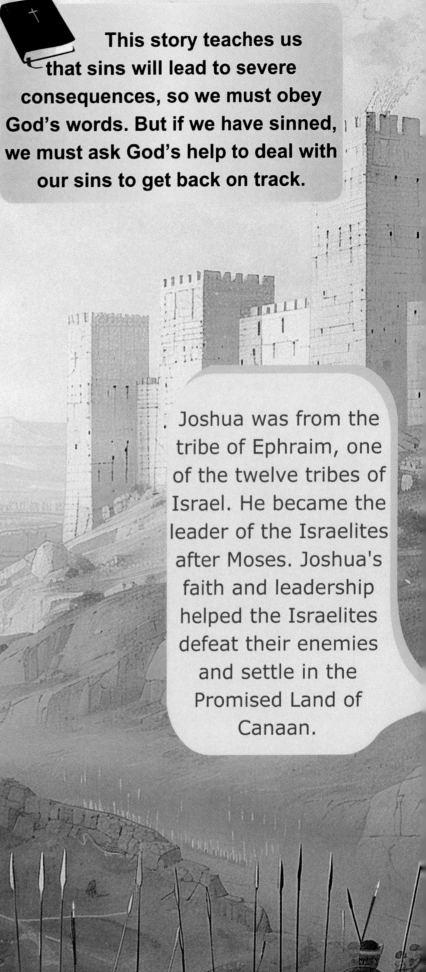

This story teaches us that we should not be afraid of feeling weak or unqualified. Instead, we should always ask for God's power to rest on us.

Gideon's Victory
(Judges 6-7)

God heard the Israelites crying for help, so He chose Gideon to save them from their oppressors the Midianites. Although feeling weak and unqualified for the job, Gideon obeyed God's plan and surrounded the enemy camp with just three hundred men. During the night, they used torches and trumpets to create confusion. As a result, the Midianite soldiers began to kill each other in turmoil, giving Israel a miraculous win.

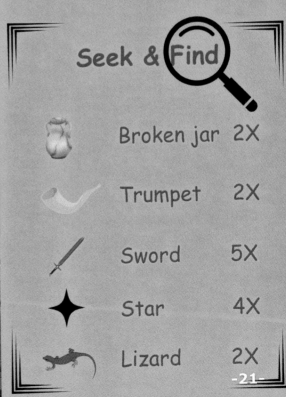

Seek & Find

	Broken jar	2X
	Trumpet	2X
	Sword	5X
	Star	4X
	Lizard	2X

Ruth's Loyalty
(Ruth 1-4)

Ruth, a Moabite woman, showed great loyalty to her mother-in-law Naomi after they both lost their husbands. Instead of staying in her hometown Moab, Ruth comforted Naomi and traveled with her back to Bethlehem, as Naomi was an Israelite. Ruth's hard work and dedication won her a great reputation in Bethlehem, which led to her marriage to Boaz and becoming part of the family line of King David.

Ruth was a Gentile woman from Moab, but her life was redeemed, and she was placed in the Messianic line as the great-grandmother of King David and an ancestor of Jesus Christ.

Seek & Find

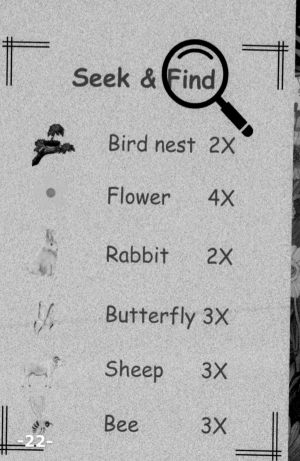

Bird nest	2X
Flower	4X
Rabbit	2X
Butterfly	3X
Sheep	3X
Bee	3X

This story teaches us about love and redemption. It shows God's gracious provision where broken people are made whole, and sinful people are forgiven.

This story teaches us that when we face the 'Goliaths' in our lives, we will fear no more if we see them through God, as God will give us strength and victory.

David was from the tribe of Judah, one of Israel's twelve tribes. David later became a great king of Israel and was the great-grandson of Ruth.

David and Goliath
(1 Samuel 17)

During the ancient war between Israel and the Philistines, a giant soldier named Goliath challenged the Israelites to a one-on-one fight. Fearful of his size, no one from Israel stepped up until a young shepherd named David volunteered. Armed with just a sling and five stones but with strong faith in God, David killed Goliath, enabling Israel to turn on the Philistines for a complete victory.

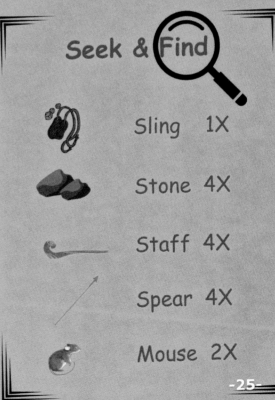

Seek & Find

	Sling	1X
	Stone	4X
	Staff	4X
	Spear	4X
	Mouse	2X

Solomon Builds the Temple
(1 Kings 6-8)

King Solomon spent seven years building a magnificent temple in Jerusalem as a house for God and a place of worship. The temple included significant areas such as the Holy of Holies, the Holy Place, and the Porch, as well as important features like the Bronze Altar in the courtyard. King Solomon held a grand dedication ceremony for the temple, emphasizing the covenant and praying for God's blessings.

This story teaches us that we should always make our best efforts to honor and worship God, listen to what He says, and ask for His blessings.

Seek & Find

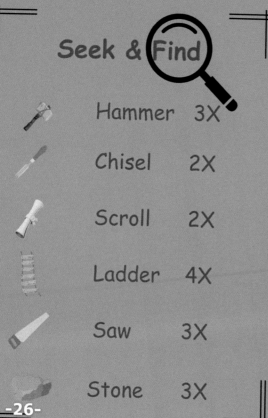

Hammer	3X
Chisel	2X
Scroll	2X
Ladder	4X
Saw	3X
Stone	3X

King Solomon, known for his wisdom, was the son of King David. He led the Kingdom of Israel to its greatest glory. However, the kingdom began to face some problems in his old age.

This story teaches us that we should not let our judgment come in the way of who deserves God's mercy, as our Lord gives mercy to all people.

Jonah was a prophet in the northern kingdom of Israel and was from the tribe of Zebulun. His name means 'Dove,' and he was known for delivering God's messages to people.

Jonah and the Whale
(Jonah 1-4)

God told Jonah to go to Nineveh to warn the people about their evil deeds. But Jonah refused and took a ship heading for the opposite direction. God stirred up a huge storm, and Jonah was thrown overboard and swallowed by a whale. Jonah realized his mistake in the whale's belly, and God had the whale spit him out so he could complete his task. As a result, the people of Nineveh heard God's words and changed their ways.

Seek & Find

Scroll	1X
Fish	4X
Crab	4X
Shell	4X
Lizard	3X
Flower	4X

Daniel in the Lion's Den

(Daniel 6)

After the Kingdom of Israel fell, many Israelites were taken to other countries. Daniel, a faithful servant of God, became a high-ranking official in the Persian Empire. Some people got Daniel into trouble, so he was thrown into the lion's den. But God sent an angel to shut the lions' mouths and Daniel was not harmed. The king then declared that everyone should worship Daniel's God.

This story teaches us that we should serve God no matter where we are and trust that He will always protect us from any danger.

Seek & Find

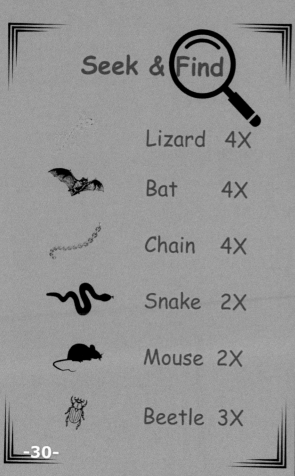

Lizard 4X

Bat 4X

Chain 4X

Snake 2X

Mouse 2X

Beetle 3X

-32-

Esther Saves Her People
(Esther 1-10)

In Susa, the capital of the Persian Empire, a Jewish woman named Esther was chosen to be the queen of Persia. An official named Haman plotted to kill all the Israelites. With the help of her cousin Mordecai, Esther bravely approached King Xerxes and cleverly exposed Haman's plan. The king was furious and ordered Haman to be punished, saving all the Jewish people.

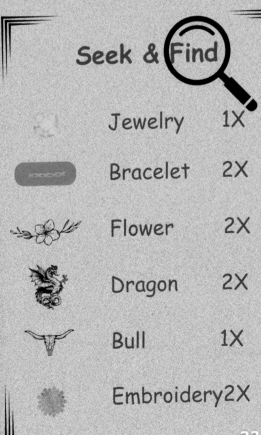

Seek & Find

	Jewelry	1X
	Bracelet	2X
	Flower	2X
	Dragon	2X
	Bull	1X
	Embroidery	2X

Answer Page

Creation Story

Noah's Ark

Abraham's Journey

Jacob's Ladder

Joseph Interprets Pharaoh's Dreams

Moses and the Burning Bush

The Conquest of Ai

Answer Page

Gideon's Victory

Ruth's Loyalty

David and Goliath

Solomon Builds the Temple

Jonah and the Whale

Daniel in the Lion's Den

Esther Saves Her People

Twelve Tribes of Israel Symbols

Reuben

Reuben was the firstborn son of Jacob. He was known for his impulsiveness and his tribe's symbol is mandrake plant.

Gad

Gad was Jacob's seventh son, His tribe was known for its bravery in battle. His tribe's symbol is a military tent.

Simeon

Simeon was Jacob's second son. He was known for his fierce and zealous nature. His tribe's symbol is a strong castle.

Asher

Asher was the eighth son of Jacob, He was blessed with fertile lands and abundant resources. His tribe's symbol is an olive tree with many branches.

Levi

Levi was Jacob's third son. He was chosen by God to serve as priests. His tribe's symbol is the breastplates worn by priests.

Issachar

Issachar was the ninth son of Jacob. He was known for his wisdom and understanding of the times. His tribe's symbol is a strong donkey.

Judah

Judah was the fourth son of Jacob and was the leader among his brothers. Many of Israel's kings were from Judah and lion is symbol of this tribe.

Zebulun

Zebulun was the tenth son of Jacob. His tribe was known for its commerce and sea trade. His tribe's symbol is a ship sailing on waves.

Dan

Dan was the fifth son of Jacob. The tribe of Dan was known for its skilled warriors and judges. His tribe's symbol is a serpent coiled on a set of scales.

Joseph

Joseph was the beloved son of Jacob. His two sons, **Ephraim** and **Manasseh**, each becoming the head of a tribe. The symbol for the **House of Joseph** is a sheaf of wheat.

Naphtali

Naphtali was the sixth son of Jacob, He was known for his swiftness and agility. His tribe's symbol is a deer reflecting the tribe's speed and grace.

Benjamin

Benjamin was the youngest son of Jacob. His tribe was known for its fierceness in battle. His tribe's symbol is a wolf.

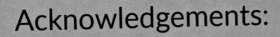

Acknowledgements:

I would like to express my heartfelt gratitude to the following individuals whose Bible teachings have deepened my understanding of God's word:

- Pastor Gary Hamrick, Cornerstone Chapel - Leesburg, VA
- Pastor Paul LeBoutillier, Calvary Chapel Ontario, Oregon

I am also deeply thankful to everyone at my local church, with special appreciation to Lily Zhou for her kind help and guidance.

A special thank you to my wife, Joling, for the unwavering support, and to my lovely son, Alex, for being the first reader and reviewer of this book.

May peace and love guide us all in our walk with the Lord.

About the Author

Jamie Whimsy writes tales that beautifully blend fantasy with reality, bringing Bible stories and Christian values to life through imaginative storytelling. As an active member of the local church, Jamie believes in the power of stories to inspire faith, teach important life lessons, and connect us all in our spiritual journey.

Discover more interactive content on Jamie's social channels:

Instagram

Youtube

Made in United States
Orlando, FL
17 September 2024

51649742R00022